curiousabout
GIANTS
BY GINA KAMMER
AMICUS LEARNING

What are you

curious about?

Curious About is published by
Amicus Learning, an imprint of Amicus
P.O. Box 227
Mankato, MN 56002
www.amicuspublishing.us

Editor: Ana Brauer
Series Designer: Kathleen Petelinsek
Book Designer and Photo Researcher: Kim Pfeffer

Library of Congress Cataloging-in-Publication Data
Names: Kammer, Gina, author.
Title: Curious about giants / by Gina Kammer.
Description: Mankato, MN : Amicus Learning, [2025] | Series:
Curious about mythical creatures | Includes bibliographical
references and index. | Audience: Ages 6–9 years | Audience:
Grades 2–3 | Summary: "Do giants have magic powers? Learn
about the Greek and Norse mythology surrounding giants in
this question-and-answer book for elementary readers. Includes
infographics, table of contents, glossary, books and websites for
further research, and index"— Provided by publisher.
Identifiers: LCCN 2024017577 (print) | LCCN 2024017578
(ebook) | ISBN 9798892000963 (lib. bdg.) | ISBN
9798892001540 (paperback) | ISBN 9798892002127 (ebook)
Subjects: LCSH: Giants (Folklore)—Juvenile literature.
Classification: LCC GR560 .K36 2025 (print) | LCC GR560
(ebook) | DDC 398.21—dc23/eng/20240531
LC record available at https://lccn.loc.gov/2024017577
LC ebook record available at https://lccn.loc.gov/2024017578

Photos © Adobe Stock/furyon, 18–19, Massimo Todaro, 9;
Alamy Stock Photo/Chris Hellier, 15; Dreamstime/Galexi, 5;
Freepik/ 4zevar, 9, meghla587, cover, n.style, 9, rawpixel.
com, 17, redwooddigitalart, 5; Getty Images/BibleArtLibrary, 5,
whitemay, 4; Shutterstock/Daniel Eskridge, 7, Michael Rosskothen,
5, Obsidian Fantasy Studio, 6; Wikimedia Commons/BenAveling,
16, George Catlin, 5, John Charles Dollman, 11, Mårten Eskil
Winge, 12–13, Public Domain, 20–21

Printed in China

Are giants real?

Yes and no. We have **proof** that some people can grow super tall. They may be called giants. But no one living has seen giants from **legends**, such as the Gigantes of Greek **myths** or the Jotun of Norse myths. Yet giants are in many stories!

NATIVE AMERICAN (CHOCTAW): WHITE GIANTS
GREEK: CYCLOPS
NORSE: JOTUN
GREAT BRITAIN: GOGMAGOG
CHRISTIAN: GOLIATH
GIANTS FROM DIFFERENT CULTURES

What do giants look like?

In some stories, there are giants made of stone. They can blend in with the mountains.

Humans, usually! But big. They are strong with huge muscles. In Greek myths, some have snakes for legs. Some have six arms or one hundred hands. Others only have one eye. Some are made of rock. One formed from melting ice. They wear **armor** or animal skins. Most giants look scary!

A cyclops is a giant with one eye in Greek and Roman myths.

How big are giants?

Giants are bigger than normal humans. Some make humans look like grasshoppers. Others are only a little bit taller than most people. In Norse myths, one giant was bigger than the Earth. His body became the worlds.

Ymir was the biggest giant in Norse myths.

COMPARING SIZES
Possible Heights of Famous Giants

Average human adult 6 feet (1.8 meters) tall

Paul Bunyan 7 ft (2.1 m) tall

Goliath 7–9 ft (2.1–2.7 m) tall

Gogmagog 18 ft (5.5 m) tall

Finn McCool 54 ft (16.5 m) tall

CHAPTER TWO

Do giants have magical powers?

In myths, a giant is often like a god. They are usually closely tied to places. Some even get power from the Earth. Some created lands. A cyclops is a giant that can make lightning bolts and magic weapons.

One giant from Norse myths uses a flaming blade.

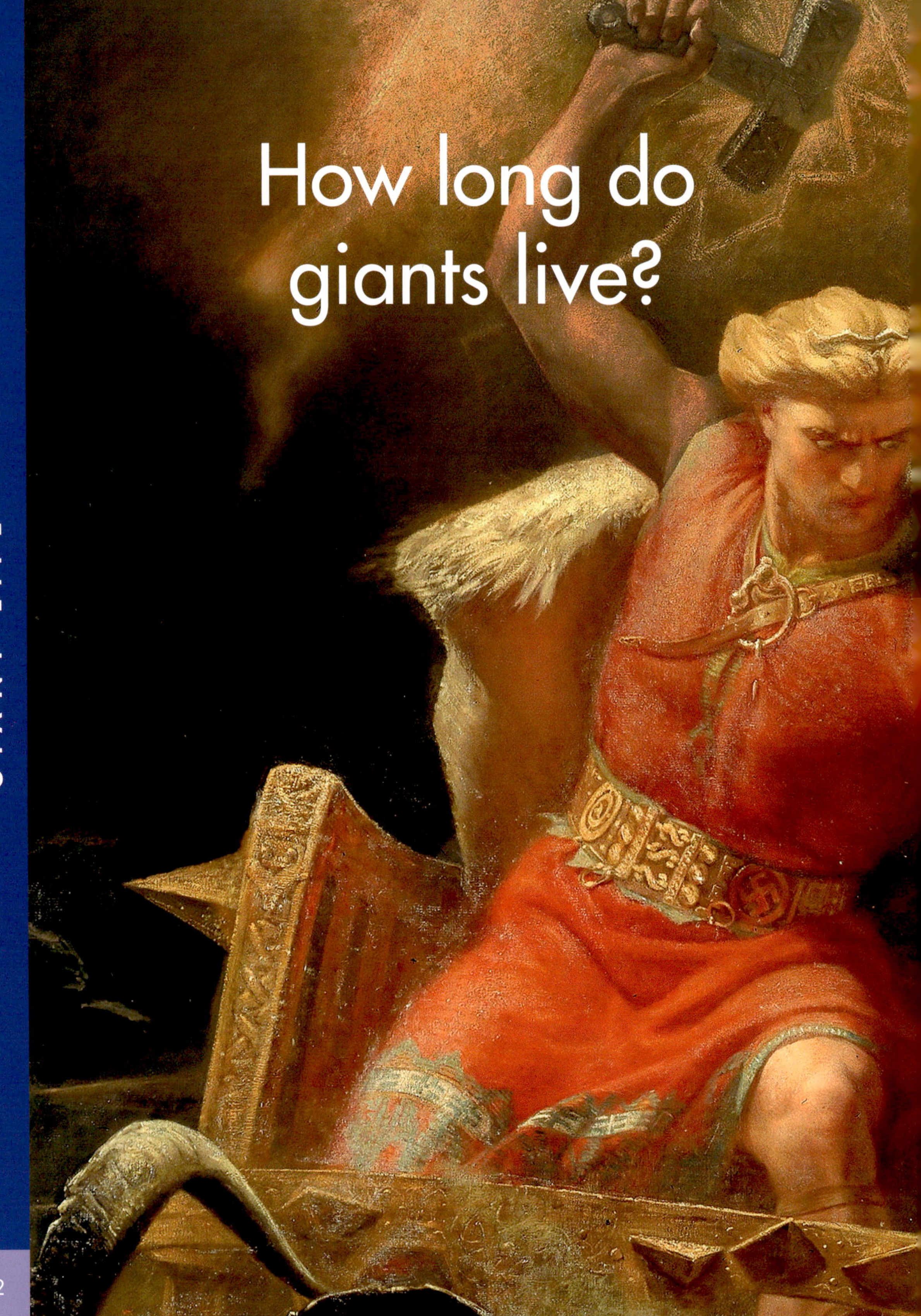
How long do giants live?

Some live as long as humans. But they might have shorter lives. They get into fights. Some are killed. Others are said to live forever! In one legend, a giant's heart is made of ice. A girl's kindness helps melt his heart. Then he turns back into a normal man.

In Norse myths, Thor was an enemy of giants. They would often get into fights.

Are giants friendly?

Not usually. In most legends, giants are known to eat people. In some myths, "giant" comes from a word that means "**devourer**." At the very least, giants are dangerous around humans. They might step on someone and not know it!

In many legends, giants will fight
humans without a reason.

CHAPTER THREE

Where do giants live?

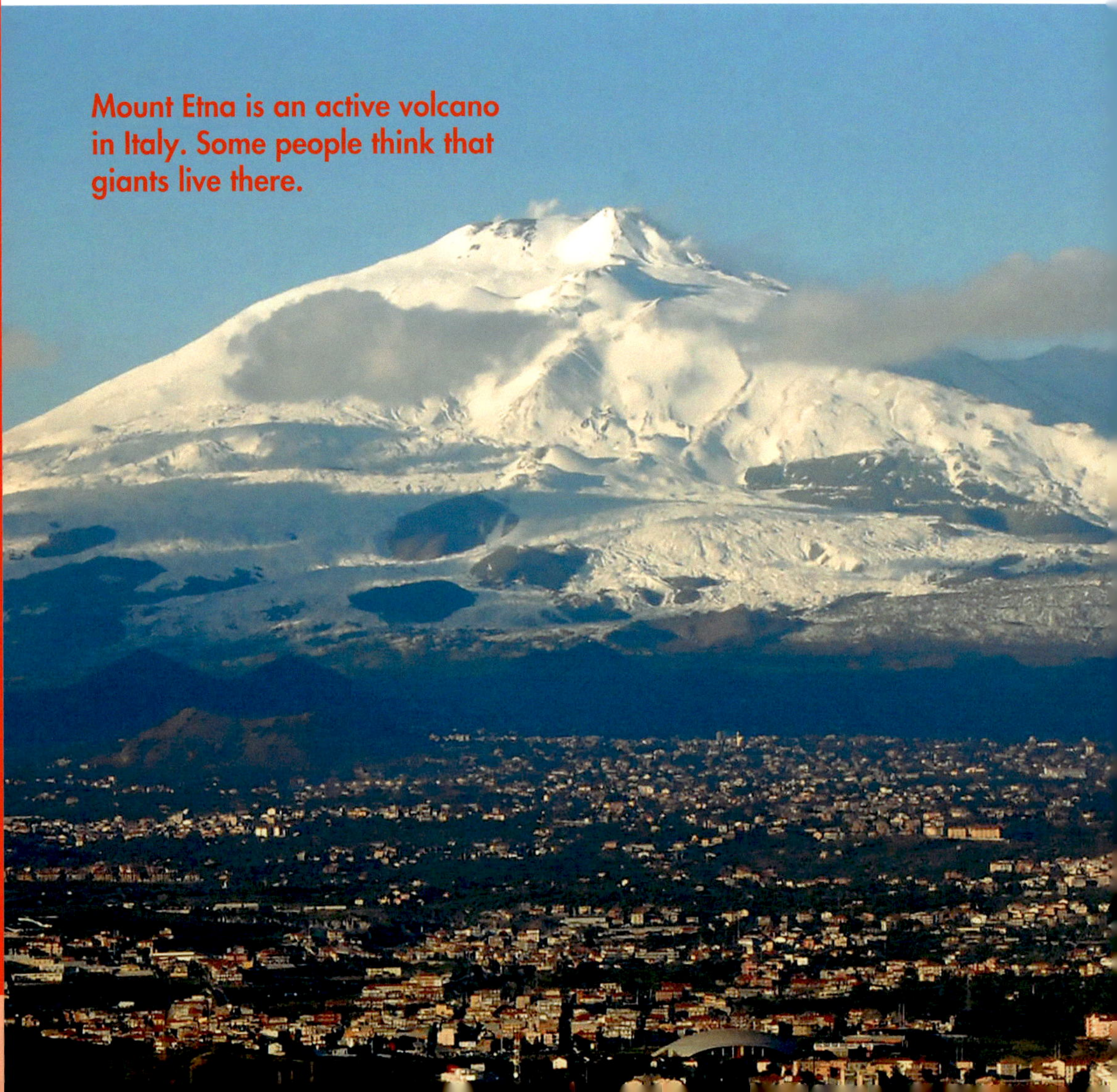

Mount Etna is an active volcano in Italy. Some people think that giants live there.

All over the world! Most cultures have stories about giants living there. But giants tend to live in wild places with no rules. They live on mountains or in caves. Some are said to be under volcanoes. When they move, the Earth shakes.

What hurts a giant?

Some have skin like rock. Giants are tough! But a slingshot or arrows have worked in the past. People can stay far enough away so they don't get squashed! In some myths, showing them a little kindness first works better.

What else could giants be?

Maybe they are just tall people! Some people are born with **gigantism**. It makes them grow faster than others. Some ancient warriors were strong and fierce. Their enemies thought they seemed larger than they really were. Or people found large bones. They thought the bones must have been from giants.

At 8 ft. 11 in. (2.72 m),
Robert Wadlow was the
tallest person to ever live.

ASK MORE QUESTIONS

What stories have people told about giants?

Who were some famous giants in legends?

Try a BIG QUESTION: Why do people believe giants were real?

SEARCH FOR ANSWERS

Search the library catalog or the Internet.
A librarian, teacher, or parent can help you.

Using Keywords
Find the looking glass.

Keywords are the most important words in your question.

If you want to know about:

- Giants in legends, type: GIANT LEGENDS

- other Greek myths, type: GREEK MYTHOLOGY

FIND GOOD SOURCES

Are the sources reliable?

Some sources are better than others. An adult can help you. Here are some good, safe sources.

Books

Giants
by Martha London, 2020.

Giants: Fairy Tale Creatures
by Mark L. Lewis, 2022.

Internet Sites

Aquila: Giants in Mythology
https://blog.aquila.co.uk/giants-in-mythology-and-fiction/
Aquila is a children's magazine written by experts.

Britannica Kids: Paul Bunyan
https://kids.britannica.com/kids/article/Paul-Bunyan/351398
Britannica is an encyclopedia with educational information on many topics.

SHARE AND TAKE ACTION

Take a walk around your neighborhood with an adult.

What kinds of giants can you find? Giant trees? Fields? Buildings? Something else? Imagine a giant created it, and share your tall tale.

Ask an adult to measure how tall you are.

Figure out how many of you would need to stand on your shoulders to be taller than a giant.

What animals live in wild places?

Find out what lives in the places giants might have been.

GLOSSARY

armor A covering to protect something.

devourer One that eats greedily.

gigantism A condition where someone grows to a much larger than average size.

legend A story from the past that may or may not be true but cannot be checked.

monument A stone, statue, or building to mark something.

myth An idea or story that is believed by many people but that is not true.

proof Evidence of something.

INDEX

About the Author

Gina Kammer grew up writing and illustrating her own stories. Now she teaches others to write stories at inkybookwyrm.com. She likes reading fantasy and medieval literature. She also enjoys traveling, oil painting, archery, and snuggling her grumpy bunny. She lives in Minnesota.